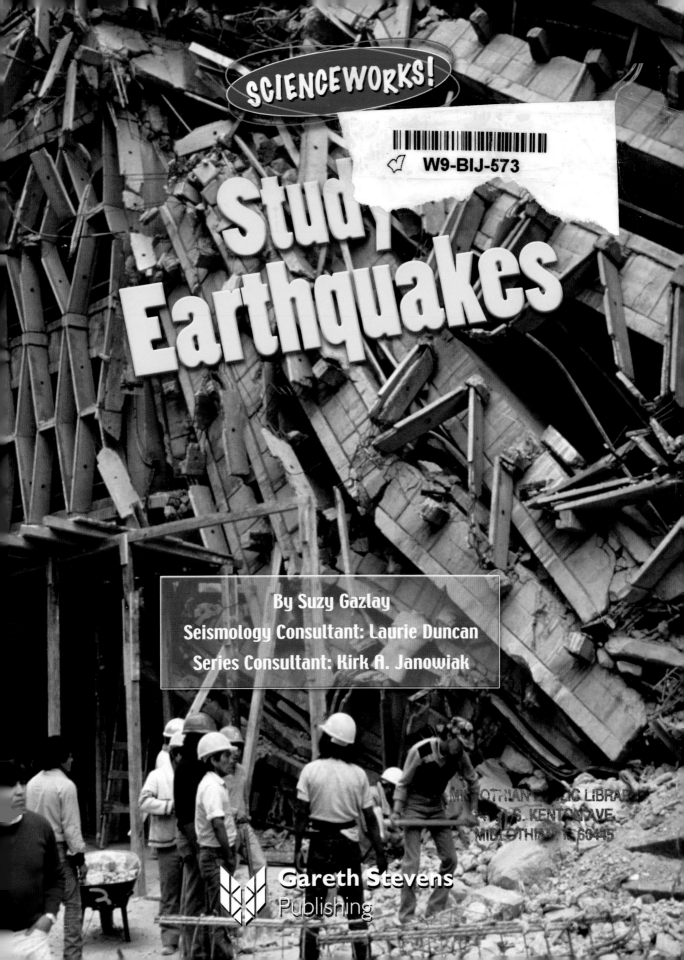

SCIENCEWORKS!

Study Earthquakes

By Suzy Gazlay

Seismology Consultant: Laurie Duncan

Series Consultant: Kirk A. Janowiak

Gareth Stevens
Publishing

Please visit our web site at www.garethstevens.com. For a free catalog describing our list of high-quality books, call 1-800-542-2595 (USA) or 1-800-387-3178 (Canada). Our fax: 1-877-542-2596

Library of Congress Cataloging-in-Publication Data available upon request from publisher.
ISBN-13: 978-0-8368-8931-4 (lib. bdg.)
ISBN-10: 0-8368-8931-2 (lib. bdg.)
ISBN-13: 978-0-8368-8938-3 (softcover)
ISBN-10: 0-8368-8938-X (softcover)

This North American edition first published in 2008 by
Gareth Stevens Publishing
A Weekly Reader® Company
1 Reader's Digest Road
Pleasantville, NY 10570-7000 USA

This U.S. edition copyright © 2008 by Gareth Stevens, Inc. Original edition copyright © 2007 by ticktock Media Ltd.
First published in Great Britain in 2007 by ticktock Media Ltd., Unit 2, Orchard Business Centre, North Farm Road,
Tunbridge Wells, Kent, TN2 3XF United Kingdom

ticktock Project Editor: Joe Harris
ticktock Designer: James Powell
With thanks to: Sara Greasley

Gareth Stevens Editor: Jayne Keedle
Gareth Stevens Creative Director: Lisa Donovan
Gareth Stevens Graphic Designer: Keith Plechaty

Printed in the United States of America

1 2 3 4 5 6 7 8 9 10 09 08 07

SUZY GAZLAY

Suzy Gazlay (M.A. Integrated Math/Science Education) is a teacher and writer who has worked with students of all ages. She has also served as a science specialist, curriculum developer, and consultant in varying capacities. She is the recipient of a Presidential Award for Excellence in Math and Science Teaching. Now retired from full-time classroom teaching, she continues to write, consult, and work with educators and children, particularly in science and music education. Her many interests include music, environmental issues, marine biology, and the outdoors.

KIRK A. JANOWIAK

Kirk A. Janowiak (B.S. Biology & Natural Resources, M.S. Ecology & Animal Behavior, M.S. Science Education) has enjoyed teaching students from pre-school through college. He has been awarded the National Association of Biology Teachers' Outstanding Biology Teacher Award and was honored to be a finalist for the Presidential Award for Excellence in Math & Science Teaching. Kirk currently teaches Biology and Environmental Science and enjoys a wide range of interests from music to the art of roasting coffee.

LAURIE DUNCAN

Laurie Duncan (Ph.D. Marine Geology and Geophysics) is a geology professor and science writer in Austin, Texas. Some of her research interests include seafloor mapping, active faults and earthquakes, plate tectonic boundaries, ocean currents and global sea level rise since the last ice age. In addition to teaching and writing about geology, nature and the outdoors, Laurie is interested in environmental policy issues. She is also an avid cyclist, rock climber and sometime mountaineer.

CONTENTS

This book will help students develop these vital science skills:

- Asking questions about objects, organisms, and events in the environment
- Employing simple equipment and tools to gather data and extend the senses
- Using data to construct a reasonable explanation
- Communicating investigations and explanations
- Understanding properties of objects and materials
- Identifying position and motion of objects
- Identifying a simple problem
- Proposing a solution
- Implementing proposed solutions
- Communicating a problem, design, and solution
- Understanding science and technology
- Distinguishing between natural objects and objects made by humans
- Understanding personal health
- Identifying changes in environments
- Using science and technology in local challenges

Supports the National Science Education Standards (NSES) for Grades K–4

HOW TO USE THIS BOOK

Science is important in the lives of people everywhere. We use science at home and at school. In fact, we use science all the time. You need to know science to understand how the world works. A seismologist is an earthquake scientist. Seismologists use science to measure the effects of earthquakes. They also use science to predict earthquakes, landslides, and tsunamis. With this book, you will use science to help leaders prepare their city for a major earthquake!

This exciting science book is very easy to use. Check out what's inside!

INTRODUCTION

Do you have what it takes to be a seismologist? Find out as you study earthquakes!

FACTFILE

Read easy-to-understand information about how and why earthquakes happen.

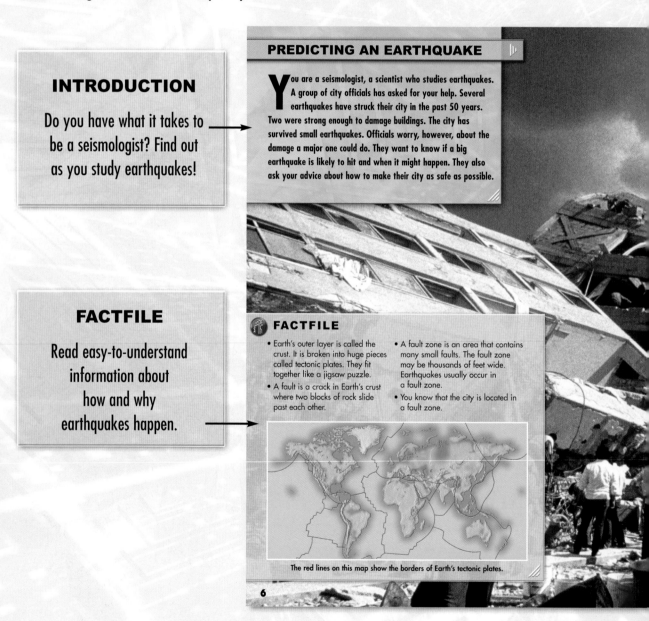

PREDICTING AN EARTHQUAKE

You are a seismologist, a scientist who studies earthquakes. A group of city officials has asked for your help. Several earthquakes have struck their city in the past 50 years. Two were strong enough to damage buildings. The city has survived small earthquakes. Officials worry, however, about the damage a major one could do. They want to know if a big earthquake is likely to hit and when it might happen. They also ask your advice about how to make their city as safe as possible.

FACTFILE

- Earth's outer layer is called the crust. It is broken into huge pieces called tectonic plates. They fit together like a jigsaw puzzle.
- A fault is a crack in Earth's crust where two blocks of rock slide past each other.

- A fault zone is an area that contains many small faults. The fault zone may be thousands of feet wide. Earthquakes usually occur in a fault zone.
- You know that the city is located in a fault zone.

The red lines on this map show the borders of Earth's tectonic plates.

6

WORKSTATION

Learn how scientists interpret earthquake data using diagrams, charts, graphs, and maps.

CHALLENGE QUESTIONS

Now that you understand the science, put it into practice.

This image shows the destruction caused by an earthquake in Mexico in 1985. This is the kind of damage a big quake could do to the city you are helping.

WORKSTATION

What Is an Earthquake?

An earthquake is a sudden movement in Earth's crust. A quake occurs when two tectonic plates slip past each other.

fault

tectonic plates

seismic waves

- As plates try to slide past each other, they get stuck. Pressure builds up at their edges.

- The plates suddenly jerk into a new position. This creates vibrations called seismic waves.

How Plates Move

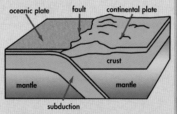

oceanic plate   fault   continental plate

crust

mantle   mantle

subduction

- Earth's tectonic plates float on the top layer in the mantle. That is the main layer beneath the crust.

- Currents in the mantle cause the tectonic plates to move slowly. Sometimes they push together or pull apart. Sometimes they scrape past each other.

- One plate may force another plate to fall below it. The plate slides into the mantle. That is called subduction.

- Plate movements cause faults to form along the crust. A major movement along a fault releases seismic waves. We feel that movement as an earthquake.

Q CHALLENGE QUESTIONS

The city officials ask you some questions about earthquakes. Can you give them the right answers?

1. Why has the city suffered from earthquakes in the past?

2. What is a fault?

3. What is the movement of one plate below another called?

4. Where are earthquakes most likely to occur?

7

IF YOU NEED HELP!

TIPS FOR SCIENCE SUCCESS

On page 30 you will find lots of tips to help you with your science work.

ANSWERS

Turn to page 31 to check your answers. (*Try all the activities and questions before you take a look at the answers.*)

GLOSSARY

Turn to page 32 for definitions of earthquake science words.

PREDICTING AN EARTHQUAKE

You are a seismologist, a scientist who studies earthquakes. A group of city officials has asked for your help. Several earthquakes have struck their city in the past 50 years. Two were strong enough to damage buildings. The city has survived small earthquakes. Officials worry, however, about the damage a major one could do. They want to know if a big earthquake is likely to hit and when it might happen. They also ask your advice about how to make their city as safe as possible.

FACTFILE

- Earth's outer layer is called the crust. It is broken into huge pieces called tectonic plates. They fit together like a jigsaw puzzle.

- A fault is a crack in Earth's crust where two blocks of rock slide past each other.

- A fault zone is an area that contains many small faults. The fault zone may be thousands of feet wide. Earthquakes usually occur in a fault zone.

- You know that the city is located in a fault zone.

The red lines on this map show the borders of Earth's tectonic plates.

This image shows the destruction caused by an earthquake in Mexico in 1985. This is the kind of damage a big quake could do to the city you are helping.

What Is an Earthquake?

An earthquake is a sudden movement in Earth's crust. A quake occurs when two tectonic plates slip past each other.

fault

tectonic plates

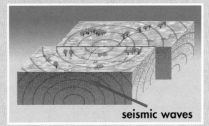
seismic waves

- As plates try to slide past each other, they get stuck. Pressure builds up at their edges.

- The plates suddenly jerk into a new position. This creates vibrations called seismic waves.

How Plates Move

- Earth's tectonic plates float on the top layer in the mantle. That is the main layer beneath the crust.
- Currents in the mantle cause the tectonic plates to move slowly. Sometimes they push together or pull apart. Sometimes they scrape past each other.

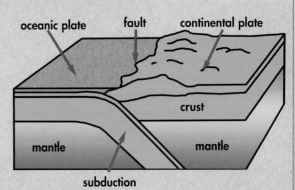
oceanic plate   fault   continental plate

crust

mantle   mantle

subduction

- One plate may force another plate to fall below it. The plate slides into the mantle. That is called subduction.
- Plate movements cause faults to form along the crust. A major movement along a fault releases seismic waves. We feel that movement as an earthquake.

Q CHALLENGE QUESTIONS

The city officials ask you some questions about earthquakes. Can you give them the right answers?

1. Why has the city suffered from earthquakes in the past?

2. What is a fault?

3. What is the movement of one plate below another called?

4. Where are earthquakes most likely to occur?

7

You need the latest and most accurate information about earthquakes. You find it at the National Geophysical Data Center (NGDC) in Boulder, Colorado. A map on a wall at the NGDC shows the locations of the most powerful earthquakes since 1900. You're not surprised to see three in Indonesia, a country in Southeast Asia. Indonesia is located in the Ring of Fire, a very active fault zone in the Pacific.

Inside an Earthquake

During an earthquake, seismic waves spread out from a point deep underground. That point is called the focus. The strongest shaking happens at the epicenter. That is the area directly above the focus.

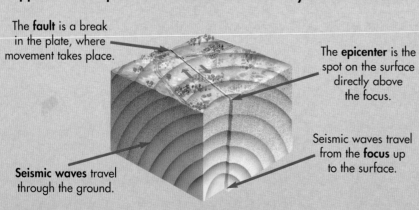

The **fault** is a break in the plate, where movement takes place.

The **epicenter** is the spot on the surface directly above the focus.

Seismic waves travel from the **focus** up to the surface.

Seismic waves travel through the ground.

This photo shows the San Andreas Fault in California.

WORKSTATION

There are 12 main tectonic plates and about 40 smaller ones. The red lines on this map outline the main plates. The letters show where major earthquakes have occurred.

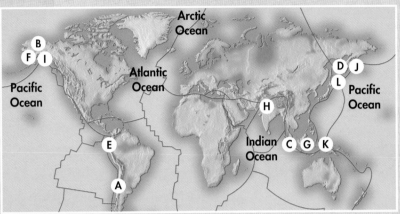

The strength and size of an earthquake are described by its magnitude. Magnitude is a measure of the total energy of an earthquake. This is calculated using the Moment Magnitude Scale.

THE MOST POWERFUL EARTHQUAKES SINCE 1900		
Location	Magnitude	Date
A Chile, South America	9.5	May 22, 1960
B Alaska, United States	9.2	March 28, 1964
C Indonesia, Asia	9.1	December 26, 2004
D Kamchatka, Russia	9.0	November 4, 1952
E Ecuador, South America	8.8	January 31, 1906
F Alaska, United States	8.7	February 4, 1965
G Indonesia, Asia	8.7	March 28, 2005
H India-China border, Asia	8.6	August 15, 1950
I Alaska, United States	8.6	March 9, 1957
J Kamchatka, Russia	8.5	February 3, 1923
K Indonesia, Asia	8.5	February 1, 1938
L Kuril Islands (Russia/Japan)	8.5	October 13, 1963

Q CHALLENGE QUESTIONS

1. What is the spot on the surface directly above an earthquake called?

2. What scale do scientists use to measure the strength of an earthquake?

3. Look at the chart above. Which was the strongest earthquake since 1900?

4. How many quakes measured 9.0 or more?

5. The most major earthquakes happen in and around which ocean?

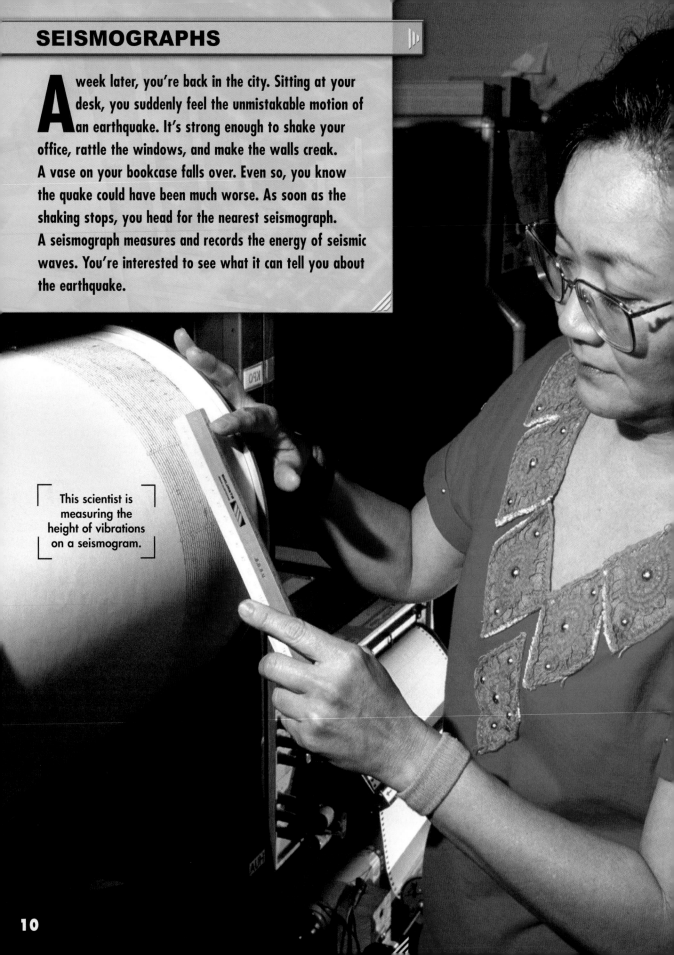

SEISMOGRAPHS

A week later, you're back in the city. Sitting at your desk, you suddenly feel the unmistakable motion of an earthquake. It's strong enough to shake your office, rattle the windows, and make the walls creak. A vase on your bookcase falls over. Even so, you know the quake could have been much worse. As soon as the shaking stops, you head for the nearest seismograph. A seismograph measures and records the energy of seismic waves. You're interested to see what it can tell you about the earthquake.

This scientist is measuring the height of vibrations on a seismogram.

Two types of seismic waves move inside the ground.

PRIMARY, OR P WAVES

SECONDARY, OR S WAVES

- Primary, or P, waves are the first waves that people feel. They travel fastest and arrive first. P waves push and pull the ground back and forth.

- P waves are followed by secondary, or S, waves. S waves move the ground up and down and from side to side.

- Surface waves travel on top of the ground. They arrive after P and S waves and move more slowly.

This is the seismogram for the earthquake you just felt.

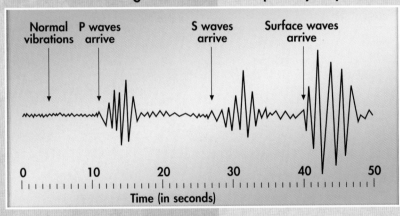

Normal vibrations

P waves arrive

S waves arrive

Surface waves arrive

0   10   20   30   40   50

Time (in seconds)

- A seismogram is a printed record from a seismograph.

- The up and down lines show vibrations. The more jagged they are, the stronger the quake.

- Different kinds of seismic waves travel at different speeds and arrive at different times.

Q CHALLENGE QUESTIONS

You look closely at the seismogram.

1. Which kind of waves caused the strongest vibrations?

2. At what point (in seconds) did the first P waves arrive?

3. How many seconds after the first P waves did the first S waves arrive?

4. How many seconds after the first P waves did the first surface waves arrive?

FINDING THE EPICENTER

You want to find the epicenter of the earthquake. Was it within the city, or did the shaking you felt come from a break somewhere else along the fault? To find out, you need two more seismograms of the same quake recorded at other locations nearby. You ask nearby scientists to send you their readings. Now that you have three seismograms, you can pinpoint the exact epicenter.

FACTFILE

Your seismograph looks like the one below.

- When the ground shakes, the base and the drum move back and forth. The hanging weight stays still.

- As the base moves, the pen writes on the drum. It draws the zigzag lines you see on the seismogram.

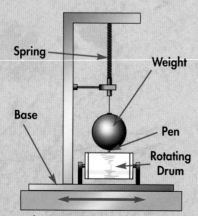

Horizontal movement caused by seismic waves

The epicenter will be found somewhere along the line of the fault.

To find the epicenter, you study the seismic waves recorded by the seismograph.

- You measure the difference between the arrival times of the P waves and S waves. The farther you are from the epicenter, the longer the time between the P waves and S waves.

- You figure out how many miles the epicenter was from your location. But you only know the distance not the exact location. To find the epicenter, you use the data collected by the other two seismographs.

- The map below shows the locations of all three seismographs (S1, S2, and S3). You draw a circle around each location to mark its distance to the epicenter. You find a place where all three rings cross. That is the epicenter of the earthquake!

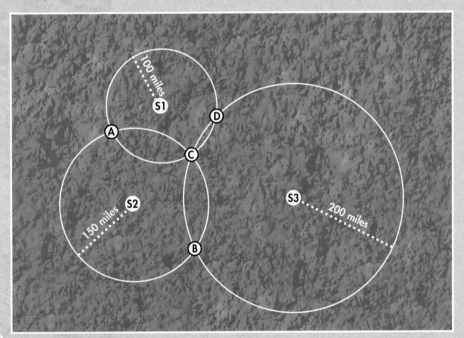

Q CHALLENGE QUESTIONS

1. Which part of a seismograph stays still during an earthquake?

2. Look at the map above. Which point marks the epicenter of the earthquake: A, B, C or D?

3. Which of the three seismographs is closest to the epicenter?

4. How far is S2 from the epicenter?

During the next few days, you talk to many people. Some were near the epicenter of the quake. Others were as far away as several hundred miles. You ask them where they were when the quake hit. You want to know what they experienced. You get many different answers!

A "Bottles and cans came crashing off the high shelves. The big front window cracked."

Alice, shopper, in market

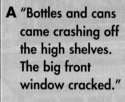

B "The windows creaked and the room shook a little. I thought I saw my lunch tray move."

Ben, student, in classroom

C "Everyone ran outside. The old brick building next door was pretty badly damaged."

Chantrelle, accountant, in office

D "I felt it, but it wasn't very strong. I thought it was a big truck going by."

Dan, trainer, in gym

E "A few cars almost skidded off the road. The only damage I saw was a chimney that fell down."

Eddie, police officer, on street

F "I didn't feel a thing. I didn't even know about it until I heard about it later."

Frederico, mechanic, in garage

WORKSTATION

Measuring Magnitude

An earthquake can be measured by its magnitude. That tells how much energy it releases. It can also be described by its intensity. That is the strength of shaking at a certain location. Intensity is measured by the Modified Mercalli Intensity Scale. This scale is used to describe the effects of an earthquake.

• An earthquake gets weaker, or has less intensity, farther from the epicenter.

• The magnitude of an earthquake is the same no matter where you are.

	MODIFIED MERCALLI INTENSITY SCALE	Magnitude Scale
I	Vibrations detected only by sensitive instruments.	1.5
II	Vibrations are felt by some people, especially on upper floors. Hanging objects may swing.	2
III	Vibrations felt noticeably indoors, but not always recognized as an earthquake. The vibrations feel similar to a passing truck.	2.5
IV	Many people indoors, but few outdoors, feel the vibrations. Dishes, windows, and doors move. Cars rock noticeably.	3 / 3.5
V	Felt by most people. Dishes, windows, and plaster may break. Tall objects sway.	4
VI	Felt by everyone. Many people are frightened and run outdoors. Damage is small.	4.5
VII	Everybody runs outdoors. Damage to buildings varies, depending on the quality of construction. The vibrations are felt by people driving cars.	5
VIII	Walls, monuments, and chimneys may fall. Drivers have trouble controlling cars.	5.5
IX	Cracks appear in buildings. The ground cracks and underground pipes are broken.	6 / 6.5
X	Most brick and wooden buildings are destroyed. Rails bend, and landslides happen.	7
XI	Few buildings remain standing. Bridges are destroyed, and cracks open in the ground. Pipes are broken.	7.5
XII	Total destruction. The ground seems to move like a wave. Objects are thrown into the air.	8

Q CHALLENGE QUESTION

Six people (pictured at left) described the effects of the earthquake. Based on that information, give each person a Mercalli number from I to XII.

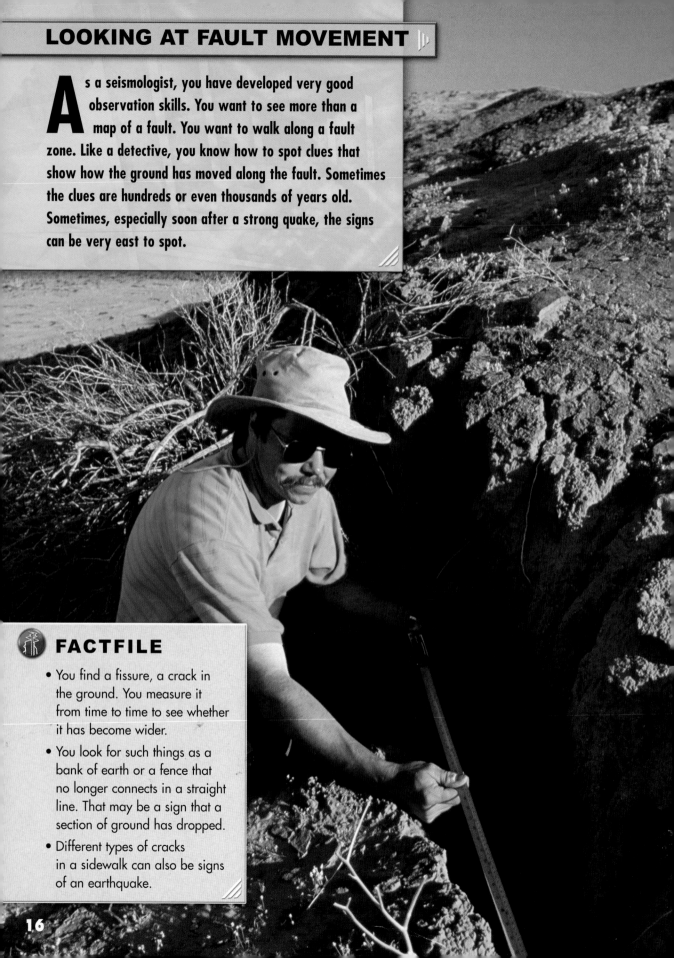

LOOKING AT FAULT MOVEMENT ⏵

As a seismologist, you have developed very good observation skills. You want to see more than a map of a fault. You want to walk along a fault zone. Like a detective, you know how to spot clues that show how the ground has moved along the fault. Sometimes the clues are hundreds or even thousands of years old. Sometimes, especially soon after a strong quake, the signs can be very east to spot.

FACTFILE

- You find a fissure, a crack in the ground. You measure it from time to time to see whether it has become wider.

- You look for such things as a bank of earth or a fence that no longer connects in a straight line. That may be a sign that a section of ground has dropped.

- Different types of cracks in a sidewalk can also be signs of an earthquake.

There are two basic types of movement along a fault.

STRIKE-SLIP MOVEMENT

- The most common type is sideways, or strike-slip movement. The movement can be either to the right or to the left.

- Movement along a fault can also be up or down. That is known as dip-slip movement. If one side of the fault drops down, it's called a normal fault. If one side is pushed up over the other side, it's called a thrust fault. Either way, one side of the fault ends up higher than the other.

DIP-SLIP MOVEMENT

NORMAL FAULT

DIP-SLIP MOVEMENT

THRUST FAULT

Q CHALLENGE QUESTIONS

Look at these photos that show fault movement. Which ones show strike-slip movement? Which ones show dip-slip movement?

1

2

3

4

DIGGING INTO THE FAULT

To get firsthand information about a fault, you want to go inside it. You join other scientists in a trench that has been dug across a fault. Down inside, you take a close look at the fault. You also study the smaller faults that connect to it. You want to measure and identify the different types of rock you see. Most of all, you want to find out about past movement along this section of the fault.

FACTFILE

- Digging into a trench is like digging into history. The deeper you dig, the further you travel into the past.
- You can use information about past quakes to predict when the next quake might hit. You can also use it to predict where, and how big, the next quake might be.

800

WORKSTATION

You watch as a backhoe digs the trench.

- You are eager to climb down and take measurements, samples, and pictures.
- You discover that the most recent major earthquake happened 780 years ago.

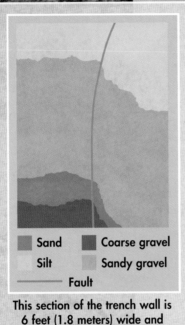

Sand
Silt
Coarse gravel
Sandy gravel
—— Fault

This section of the trench wall is 6 feet (1.8 meters) wide and 10 feet (3 meters) tall.

You can see when earthquakes happened by looking at different layers of rock in the trench wall.

- New soil and rock is added to the surface at a steady rate. Over time, different kinds of rock have settled. Each is represented in the diagram by a different color.
- You can tell that an earthquake happened when you find a sudden change in the level of the rock.
- Look at the coarse gravel layer. When this layer was on the surface, a quake happened. One side of the fault moved up, and the other moved down.
- You want to figure out how long ago an earthquake happened. You measure how much soil and rock have piled up on top of the layer where the earthquake took place.

1857

1812

1100

This scientist is pointing to a spot where an earthquake has occurred.

The labels on the wall of the trench show the dates of past earthquakes.

Q CHALLENGE QUESTIONS

This photograph shows the same section of the trench as the diagram above. Match each statement to a letter on the photograph (right).

1. An earthquake occurred in this layer.
2. This is the most recent layer.
3. This layer is made up of sand.
4. This is the line of the fault.

19

EARTHQUAKES ON THE OCEAN FLOOR

You've explored and studied faults before and after quakes. That's fairly easy to do when the fault is on land. It's harder when the fault is on the ocean floor, under several thousand feet of water! The fault that runs beneath the city also goes out to sea. To examine that section of the fault, you go on a special research ship. You watch as an engineer prepares the ship's huge hollow drill. The drill will cut out a section of the sea bed for you to study.

 FACTFILE

- The research ship is equipped with a drilling rig. The rig rises above the ship's deck like a tower.

- The ship's drill is lowered through hundreds of feet of seawater to the ocean floor.

- The drill cuts out a long column of rock material called a core. This type of drilling is like coring an apple.

- The core is transported up a pipe to the ship.

drill
sand
mud

CORE SAMPLE

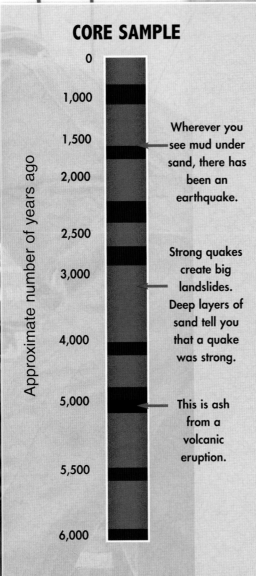

Approximate number of years ago

0
1,000
1,500
2,000
2,500
3,000
4,000
5,000
5,500
6,000

Wherever you see mud under sand, there has been an earthquake.

Strong quakes create big landslides. Deep layers of sand tell you that a quake was strong.

This is ash from a volcanic eruption.

■ Mud   ■ Sand

You and other scientists are examining a piece of core that is 8 feet (2.4 m) long.

- The core was taken from a fault zone on the seafloor, 1 mile (1.6 kilometers) below sea level.
- The core sample shows how rock materials are layered on the ocean floor. It contains sediments dating to 6,000 years ago. You notice that a pattern has been repeating over time.

The core taken from the ocean floor is brought on board the ship.

- The ocean floor is normally covered with mud. The mud is made of material that has settled on the bottom.
- When a major earthquake occurs, it triggers a landslide. Sand slides down and covers the mud.
- Over time, another layer of mud forms on top of the sand. Whenever you see mud under sand, you know there has been an earthquake.

Q CHALLENGE QUESTIONS

1. How many major earthquakes are recorded in this core?
2. How long ago was the thickest layer of sand deposited?
3. How long ago was the thinnest sand layer put down? How do you think that quake might compare to the others?
4. How long ago did the volcano erupt?

You visit the city officials to tell them what you have discovered from your research. You have learned a lot about the fault beneath their city. You tell them that your findings suggest that a serious quake could happen very soon. They will have to do everything they can to prepare the city!

If buildings are built on the wrong type of ground, their columns may sink during an earthquake.

This parking garage was destroyed by a major earthquake in California in 1994.

FACTFILE

Here are your findings:

- From your seismogram reading, you know that the city was only 100 miles (160 km) from the epicenter of a recent quake. A larger earthquake is likely to cause serious damage.

- You examined a core sample from the ocean floor. From the sample, you learned that there have been eight major earthquakes in the last 6,000 years. That means a major earthquake has happened about every 750 years.

- By digging into the fault, you discovered that the last major earthquake happened 780 years ago. That suggests that the city is overdue for another major quake.

You have studied how past earthquakes damaged buildings. Now you can give the city officials some advice.

- Most of the damage during a quake is caused by the ground shaking. Not all ground is alike, however, even in the same neighborhood. Some kinds of earth will shake more than others.

- Structures built on hard bedrock, such as granite, shake the least and are most likely to survive.

- Deep, loose soil shakes more than bedrock.

- The most heavily damaged buildings are often built on wet, sandy soil.

You show the officials a map of their city.

The different colors show the intensity of shaking they might expect during a major earthquake. The shaking will vary according to the type of earth material in each area.

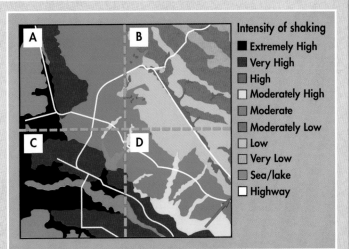

Intensity of shaking
- ■ Extremely High
- ■ Very High
- ■ High
- ☐ Moderately High
- ☐ Moderate
- ■ Moderately Low
- ☐ Low
- ☐ Very Low
- ■ Sea/lake
- ☐ Highway

Q CHALLENGE QUESTIONS

The city needs to build a new hospital. City officials ask you where would be the best place to put it.

1. Which is the best kind of ground to build on?

2. Which kind of ground is the most dangerous to build on?

3. Look at the map above. Which part of the city (A, B, C, or D) would be the best place to build the new hospital?

4. Which part of the city would be the most dangerous place to build it?

A BIG QUAKE STRIKES!

A year later, you return to the city to check on the earthquake preparations. You are shaken awake in the middle of the night. Your bed is moving across the floor! You hear a low rumbling that gets louder and louder. All around your hotel room, objects are crashing to the floor. The windows rattle and then shatter. An earthquake has hit! You scramble out of bed and crawl under the heavy desk in the corner. You can only hope that the building does not come down with you in it.

The earthquake causes destruction throughout the city. The building opposite your hotel collapsed and crushed a car.

Earthquake Safety Tips

You know that it's important to stay calm during an earthquake. During the past year, you visited many city schools to talk about earthquake safety. This is the advice that you give the students.

- If you are inside, duck, cover, and hold. Duck down on the floor. Take cover under a sturdy table or desk. Hold on to it in case you need to move with it. Stay away from glass, windows, and anything that might fall or break. Don't move until the shaking stops.

- If you are outside, move into an open area away from buildings and power lines. Falling power lines could kill you.

- If you are in a car, stop in a safe place, out of traffic. Stay away from bridges, tunnels, and overpasses, which might collapse. Avoid power lines, trees, or streetlights, which could fall.

- If you are in the mountains or near any cliffs, watch out for landslides and falling rocks.

Q CHALLENGE QUESTIONS

An earthquake has struck. What are the possible dangers in each picture? What might happen?

1 2 3 4 5

WAVE OF DESTRUCTION

The hotel you are staying in is on the seafront. When the shaking stops, you look out the broken window at the ocean. You know that when a strong quake (magnitude 7.5 or higher) hits near or beneath the ocean, there is the possibility of a tsunami. The water has gone out a long way, farther than at low tide. That is a sure sign that a tsunami is on its way!

The artist's impression shows what it would be like to witness a major tsunami. Luckily, the tsunami that hits your city is not this serious!

FACTFILE

- Tsunamis form when an earthquake shakes the sea bed. That sets a huge amount of water into motion.

- Waves spread out in all directions, traveling as fast as 500 miles (800 km) per hour.

- The waves out in the open ocean are often less than 3 feet (1 m) tall. As the water gets shallower, the waves get higher. When the waves reach land, they can be up to 100 feet (30 m) tall.

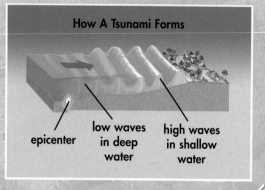

How A Tsunami Forms

epicenter   low waves in deep water   high waves in shallow water

As you watch, a high wave crashes against the shore. Luckily, the damage is not as bad as you feared. There is some flooding, but the buildings along the seafront are protected by barriers.

An average of about 10 tsunamis form every year worldwide. Most run out of energy before they reach the shore, however. The intensity of a tsunami is measured by its wave height just before it reaches the shore.

Wave Height	Effect	Frequency
1.5 feet (0.5 m)	Not noticed	Happens often
3 feet (1 m)	Low-lying coastal areas may be flooded.	Happens every four to eight months
13 feet (4 m)	Flooding, damage to buildings; Lots of litter	Happens about once a year
26 feet (8 m)	Small buildings are destroyed, and large ones are damaged. Fish are washed ashore. Some people may drown.	About once every three years
170 feet (52 m)	Nearly all buildings are totally destroyed. Trees are uprooted. Many people drown.	About once every 10 years

Number of Tsunamis Worldwide (1950 to 2000)

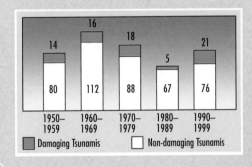

	1950–1959	1960–1969	1970–1979	1980–1989	1990–1999
Damaging Tsunamis	14	16	18	5	21
Non-damaging Tsunamis	80	112	88	67	76

Q CHALLENGE QUESTIONS

1. Look at the chart at the top of the page. How high would a tsunami wave have to be to destroy small buildings?

2. Look at the chart below it. Which 10-year period had the most tsunamis? Which period had the most damaging tsunamis? The fewest?

When you are sure the area is safe, you walk outside. Everywhere you look, there is destruction. Power lines are down, buildings have collapsed, and cars have been crushed. With a group of other scientists, you set out to view the damage. Some people have been injured, but many lives have been saved by your advice. You're pleased to hear that the new hospital was not damaged by the quake.

FACTFILE

- More than a million earthquakes happen each year, but most of them are too minor to be noticed.

- About 18 major earthquakes, with a magnitude of 7 or more, happen each year.

Your work isn't done quite yet. You inspect every damaged building to find out what went wrong.

You take a photo of each building and write a description of the damage. Sooner or later, there will be another quake. What you learn from this one will help the city do even better next time.

Q CHALLENGE QUESTIONS

Match each of the descriptions below to one of the photos above. How might this kind of damage be prevented in the future?

1. The supports of this bridge were built on soft muddy ground.

2. The walls on the bottom level of this new house were weak.

3. This bridge's supports were solid, but its design did not stand up to shaking.

4. The front wall of this building was not reinforced. It collapsed from the shaking.

Pages 8–9
Earthquakes Worldwide

The National Geophysical Data Center (NGDC) deals with all sorts of information related to studying our planet. Scientists at the center study earthquakes, volcanoes, lakes, oceans, tsunamis, climate, and natural disasters.

Pages 10–11
Seismographs

Seismograph technology has a long history. The very first seismograph was a "dragon jar" invented in China around 132 AD. The jar had eight metal dragonheads arranged around its brim. Each dragon had a ball in its mouth. Directly beneath each dragonhead was a metal open-mouthed frog. When an earthquake took place, the shaking caused a ball to drop from a dragon's mouth into the mouth of the frog.

Pages 14–15
Eyewitness Data

The Modified Mercalli Intensity Scale uses Roman numerals. This counting system was used in ancient Rome. It is easy to read once you know how. I = 1, V = 5, and X = 10. If you see a smaller number come before a larger one, subtract the smaller one from the larger one: IX = 9. Otherwise you just add them up: VI = 6. The Roman numerals on the Mercalli Scale are I (1), II (2), III (3), IV (4), V (5), VI (6), VII (7), VIII (8), IX (9), X (10), XI (11), and XII (12).

Pages 16–17
Looking at Fault Movement

Think about a road running straight across a fault line. An earthquake takes place.

- If the fault movement is strike-slip, the road on one side of the fault will move to the left and the other side will move to the right.
- If the fault movement is dip-slip, there will be a break across the road. The road on one side of the break will be higher than the road on the other side.

Pages 18–19
Digging into the Fault

Rock layers tell you if an area hasn't had earthquakes or other disturbances over the years. Such layers will look like bands of different colored rock material running sideways. If there has been an earthquake, you'll be able to see where the layers were broken and moved. In the years following the earthquake, more rock material will be deposited on top of the old layers. This gradually levels out the surface of the ground again.

Pages 20–21
Earthquakes on the Ocean Floor

The core sample shown is just one section of an entire core. You can see from the photo that an entire core is quite long—31 feet (9.4 m)! The inside of the drill pipe is lined with plastic. When the core is taken out of the pipe, the plastic wrap keeps it all together.

Pages 28–29
After the Quake

This is a big quake, but a bigger quake may still come. A quake like this one likely relieved some pressure along the fault, but pressure will continue to build. The officials always need to keep earthquakes in mind as they make decisions about the city.

Pages 6–7

1. The city has suffered from earthquakes because it is located in a fault zone.
2. A crack in Earth's crust where two blocks of rock slide past each other
3. Subduction
4. In a fault zone

Pages 8–9

1. The epicenter
2. The Moment Magnitude Scale
3. The earthquake in Chile on May 22, 1960
4. Four
5. The Pacific Ocean

Pages 10–11

1. The surface waves
2. 11 seconds
3. 16 seconds
4. 29 seconds

Pages 12–13

1. The weight
2. C
3. S1
4. 150 miles

Pages 14–15

A. Alice – V
B. Ben – IV
C. Chantrelle – VII
D. Dan – III
E. Eddie – VIII
F. Frederico – I

Pages 16–17

1. Strike-slip movement
2. Dip-slip movement
3. Dip-slip movement
4. Strike-slip movement

Pages 18–19

1. B – the coarse gravel layer
2. C – the silt layer. You can tell it is the most recent layer because it is at the top.
3. E
4. A

Pages 20–21

1. Eight major earthquakes
2. About 3,000 years ago
3. 2,500 years ago; this earthquake was probably not as strong as the others.
4. About 5,000 years ago

Pages 22–23

1. Hard bedrock, such as granite
2. Wet, sandy soil
3. Area B
4. Area C

Pages 24–25

1. There is a risk of landslides and falling rocks in the mountains and near cliffs.
2. Keep away from tunnels, which might collapse.
3. You should steer clear of power lines during an earthquake, since they could fall down and electrocute you.
4. Windows may smash during an earthquake. You could be hurt by the broken glass.
5. There is a danger that trees might fall on you during an earthquake.

Pages 26–27

1. 26 feet high
2. 1960–1969 had the most tsunamis; 1990–1999 had the most damaging tsunamis; 1980–1989 had the fewest damaging tsunamis.

Pages 28–29

1. B. In the future, bridge supports should be built on firm ground.
2. A. The walls of houses must be made of a stronger material.
3. C. Bridges must be designed to withstand shaking.
4. D. The outer walls of houses must be reinforced.

BEDROCK solid layer of rock beneath the soil

CRUST the solid outer layer of Earth that consists of landforms and the ocean floor

CURRENT the flow of a liquid or gas in one direction

EPICENTER a point on Earth's surface that is directly above the focus

FAULT a crack in Earth's crust where huge blocks of rock slide past each other

FAULT ZONE an area where many faults are connected to each other

FOCUS the point beneath Earth's surface where an earthquake begins

INTENSITY a measurement of strength; the strength of an earthquake as it is felt at the surface

MAGNITUDE a measurement of the energy released during an earthquake

MANTLE the thick layer of Earth that lies beneath the crust

MODIFIED MERCALLI INTENSITY SCALE a scale of earthquake intensity based on what people feel or see during a quake

MOMENT MAGNITUDE SCALE the scale used by scientists to measure the strength and size of an earthquake

PRESSURE A physical force put on or against an object, from something touching it

SEDIMENT sand and soil carried by water, wind, or glaciers

SEISMIC WAVES energy that ripples out from an earthquake

SEISMOGRAM a printed record of the information recorded by a seismograph

SEISMOGRAPH an instrument that detects, measures, and records vibrations in Earth at a specific location

SEISMOLOGIST a scientist who studies earthquakes, seismic waves, and the effects of earthquakes

SUBDUCTION the process in which part of a tectonic plate moves beneath another plate

TECTONIC PLATES giant pieces of Earth's crust that float on Earth's mantle. They are always moving at a very slow rate.

TSUNAMI a series of large waves caused by an earthquake or volcanic eruption beneath or close to the ocean

PICTURE CREDITS

(t = top; b = bottom; c = center; l = left; r = right)

Cover: USGS. **Corbis:** 16–17 (main), 18–19 (main). **Getty:** 8–9 (main), 25tr. **IODP/TAMU:** 20–21 (main), 20bc, 21cr. **National Oceanic and Atmospheric Administration/Department of Commerce:** 17bcl, 17bcr, 17bl, 17br, 27cl. **Rex Features:** 6–7 (main), 28–29 (main). **Royal Observatory of Belgium:** 19br. **Science Photo Library:** title page, 10–11 (main), 12–13 (main), 22–23 (main) 24–25 (main). **Shutterstock:** 14–15 (main), 14tc, 14tr, 14cl, 14c, 14bl, 14br, 25bfl, 25bl, 25bc, 25br, 25bfr, 26–27 (main), 30–31 (main). **ticktock media archive:** 6bl, 7tr, 7cr, 7tl, 8bl, 9tr, 10bl, 11tr, 11tl, 11cl, 12bl, 13bl, 17tr, 17acr, 17acl, 19cl, 20b, 21cl, 23c, 26bl, 31cr. **USGS:** cover, 19t, 23acr, 23tr, 29acl, 29acr, 29bcl, 29bcr, 30cl.

Every effort has been made to trace the copyright holders, and we apologize in advance for any unintentional omissions. We would be pleased to insert the appropriate acknowledgments in any subsequent edition of this publication.